The Reference Library in 1906, looking west

BR.......

....L CITY COL..........

LIBRARY and

CHARLES HOLDEN

A History and Guide

Anthony Beeson

Dedicated to the Shades of Dorothea Tearreau and John Herbert Beeson, my parents.

First published in 2006 by Redcliffe Press Ltd
81g Pembroke Road, Bristol BS8 3EA
www.redcliffepress.co.uk

©Bristol Libraries

ISBN 1 904537 53 7
ISBN 13 9781904537533

Published for Bristol Libraries, Bristol City Council
to mark the 100th anniversary of the opening of
Bristol Central Library, College Green, Bristol BS1 5TL
www.bristol-city.gov.uk/libraries

British Library Cataloguing in Publication Data:
A catalogue record of this book is available from the British Library

Cover and additional photography ©Stephen Morris smc@freeuk.com

Principal contemporary photography by Andrew Eason mail@andreweason.com

Designed and typeset by Stephen Morris Communications smc@freeuk.com

Printed and bound by The Charlesworth Group, Wakefield.

Thanks are expressed to the John James Foundation for their grant towards the costs of producing this book.

John James Bristol Foundation is a grant-making trust which was founded in 1983 as a result of the generosity of John James, one of Bristol's greatest philanthropists. John, though poor by birth, became one of the most dynamic and successful businessmen in post-war Britain, and the foundation which bears his name continues to centre its giving on Bristol and its residents. This approach is in keeping with John's own sentiments expressed during his lifetime, and the foundation's primary areas of focus are education, health and older people. See www.johnjames.org.uk for further information.

Contents

Public Libraries in Bristol 4

Charles Holden 9

The Structure and Building Plan 10

The Exterior 12

The Interior 20

The 1967 Extension 51

Recent Improvements 53

Further Reading 54

There are in addition eight pages of colour illustrations, to be found between pages 32-33.

Aerial view of the library in the 1920s showing the great size of the building

Public Libraries in Bristol

BRISTOL MAY LAY CLAIM to having had one of the earliest public libraries in Britain. In 1464 a library was established by John Carpenter, Bishop of Worcester, on the premises of the Guild of Kalendars. Their house was attached to the north-west corner of All Saints Church in Corn Street, the library occupying the attic above the north aisle. Carpenter's new library was based on that founded by his namesake at the Guildhall in London in 1425. Although open to the public, with two librarians who were secular priests, its stock was primarily of religious books collected mainly for the benefit of the city's clergy. That the Bristol library was planned before 1464 is evident by the bequest of a book by the dean of Westbury in 1455. At its zenith the library is said to have held an astonishing 800 volumes. The chained books were available to the public for study for two hours in the morning and two in the afternoon on weekdays and the Kalendars' prior was present in order to explain any obscure religious points. Although interested laymen might well have used the collection, it was aimed at the secular clergy while the general population was expected to benefit from it second hand through their preaching and teaching.

It is commonly believed that a fire in the church in 1464 (or 1466 according to one account) destroyed the library, although the conflagration appears to have been in the adjoining properties rather than in the church itself. On the Kalendars' dissolution in 1548, a room in the guild house was still called the library. Nicholas Orme's paper 'The Guild of Kalendars, Bristol' suggests that the real cause of the demise of the library was neglect by its keepers and public rather than conflagration.

Whether or not some variant of a public library survived in the city for the rest of the sixteenth century is unknown. In 1608 the first free public library was founded in Norwich, followed by Ipswich and then in 1613 Robert Redwood, a Bristol merchant, gave his lodge by the town wall in King Street for conversion into a library, and to accommodate the librarian. A door was cut through the town wall to allow ease of access from the city. Dr Tobias Mathew, the Bristol-born Archbishop of York, donated a substantial portion of his private library. These works, 'for the free use of the merchants and shopkeepers of the city', are still in the Reference Library collection. The vicar of St Leonard's church was appointed librarian and, from its official opening in 1615, the library flourished and was enlarged, between 1634 and 1640. 186 book chains were bought at £3 17s 6d from the ironmonger Thomas Jackson, to prevent thefts.

With funds seemingly in short supply the building became increasingly ruinous. In 1691 the Corporation considered stopping the Librarian's salary and turning most of the library into a house for letting. This did not happen, but by 1725 the Reverend Robert Clarke was petitioning for aid in repairing the unsafe structure. A committee discussed the matter for thirteen years until in 1738 it was decided to demolish the old lodge and to construct a new library on the site. Land was purchased for future expansion and hovels near the lodge demolished. For £1,301 8s 1d an elegant new building was built. The carver and architect James Paty I is credited with its design. Paty is likely to have been not only the sculptor, mason and designer but also responsible for the oak staircase with its acanthus leaf decorated treads, the book presses and elements of the fire surround in the main room on the first floor. The freestone façade of the original building is set back parallel to King Street and was originally decorated with two allegorical groups over the first floor windows representing putti studying books and the arts and sciences. The main pediment held a beautiful and superbly poised sculpture of the Bristol coat of arms. Above the gate to the courtyard an elaborate wrought-iron flambeau arch was installed at some point only to disappear in the railing stripping mania of the Second World War. The main reading room was on the first floor and approached by a staircase behind the right-hand portion of the front façade. This façade is now but a shadow of its former self as the city 'restored' it in the 1950s by slicing off and cutting back all the sculpture and mouldings.

The library developed only slowly and public lack of interest led some librarians to allow other uses to be made of parts of the building. In 1767 an important collection of books and manuscripts came to the library after the suicide of John Heylin on College Green. A meeting of various literary gentlemen in December 1772 decided to found a Subscription Library and the somewhat impertinent suggestion was made to the Corporation that it should be housed in the King Street Library to take the place of the books there 'uselessly deposited'. The City agreed, even providing financial help to repair the building. The Library Society was to prove itself a vibrant and popular institution and under its administration the King Street Library saw its most glorious literary period, with borrowers such as Samuel Taylor Coleridge, Robert Southey and Sir Humphry Davy amongst its ranks, and medieval manuscripts such as the Corporation Bible of about 1200 now found a permanent and safe home. Although there were many benefits from the formation of the Bristol Library Society, citizens unwilling or unable to pay the £4 subscription were now excluded. The free public library had disappeared, although the book stock lingered on but as a second-class alternative to the books

of the Library Society. The Society further disenfranchised the population by prohibiting anyone connected with places of entertainment, inns or lodging houses regardless of whether or not they could pay the subscription. So popular did the Library Society become and so successfully

did it accumulate new stock that a new wing was constructed at right angles to the building in 1785, consisting of a large room on the ground floor and a similar one above. These would later be turned into the Newsroom and the Reference Library of the late-Victorian institution, whilst the original Bristol Room became the Lending Library. The situation of the city's own books was made even more perilous in 1826 when the Rev Samuel Seyer, local historian and Vice-Chairman of the Society, petitioned the Council to remove their books to make way for more of the Society's. His letter was treated with contempt. Throughout this period the citizens of Bristol had paid for the maintenance of the building and assisted in other finances without benefiting.

In 1848 forty prominent Bristolians petitioned the Council to draw attention to the usurpation of public rights by a small band of private individuals and asked that the city's books should again be available to all. The Council gave the Society notice to quit. In 1855 they removed their stock to a wing of Bishop's College in Queen's Road and then in 1867 joined forces with the Bristol Philosophical Society to occupy the new Venetian Gothic building in Queen's Road in 1871 as Bristol's first museum. This was taken over by the Corporation in 1893 and the new Municipal Art Gallery opened in 1905. The reference collection of 45,000 volumes was transferred to the new Central Library in Deanery Road. The Bristol Library Society had done admirable work in building up their own stock, with the help of £14,000 of public money but with little benefit to the citizens of Bristol in the eighty years of their occupancy of King Street.

The passing of the Public Libraries Act of 1850 encouraged the Council to evict the Library Society. In 1853 the architectural firm of

Gabriel and Hirst drew up two sets of plans to adapt the King Street building to meet the requirements of the Act. Neither appear to have been acted upon but the building reopened to the public reorganised, refurbished and free on 15th September 1856. The Public Libraries Act was not officially adopted by the city until 1874, but by 1902 the city could boast not only the refurbished and renamed Central Library of 1876 in King Street, but also ten branch libraries.

The great popularity of libraries in late-Victorian Bristol put pressure on the cramped King Street premises. Plans to build a new Central Library worthy of the city foundered for lack of funds. In 1899, however, Vincent Stuckey Lean bequeathed the magnificent sum of £50,000 to Bristol for the purpose of building a new Reference Library. Lean (1820-1899) was a descendant of the Stuckey family of bankers. He had been born in Clifton and became a barrister in 1843. A bachelor, he devoted himself to the study of art, literature, natural history and travel, making a study of the world's proverbs his life's work. He amassed an impressive library at his Clevedon home which he also bequeathed to Bristol along with his legacy. With this handsome bequest (diminished by death duties to £45,000) the Corporation decided finally to build a library befitting the city's status.

In July 1901 the chosen site for the new library held the historic Old Deanery and Canons House and their gardens. The Old Deanery abutted the Abbey Gate whilst the Canons House adjoined the Victorian Tyndale Mission Hall to the west. College Green had originally been a plateau with a considerable drop to its west, now masked by the bulk of the Council House, but until the latter's construction the green was six feet higher than today, before being lowered at the architect's insistence

to improve the proportions of his building. The north wing of the Old Deanery (which had briefly functioned as the YMCA) was demolished in 1869 and a viaduct bearing what is now Deanery Road was constructed to enable traffic to reach College Green directly from the Hotwell Road. The viaduct sealed the fate of the two ancient buildings as it ran along almost at first-floor level in front of them. This site was rejected at first as being not central enough and as 'cheap and nasty' by one councillor. It was now to be rented from the Dean and Chapter for £120 per annum and the city decided to hold a competition to find the best design for the new building. At the request of the Society of Architects it was to be judged by a professional assessor, and the London architect E.W. Mountford was appointed in June 1902. The competition attracted sixty one entries. The winner was the London firm of H. Percy Adams. The *Bristol Times and Mirror* of 25th November praised the winning design but expressed doubts about the size of the main doors.

In January 1903 Percy Adams visited Bristol to go through the plans with the Library Committee. Amongst the modifications that emerged, the main entrance was to be enlarged and the whole building carried back into the garden another five feet. The work was put out to tender, and the contract was awarded to Willcock and Company of Wolverhampton whose tender was the lowest of the nine at £29,675. They agreed to employ local labour. During the demolition of the Old Deanery and the Canons House an exceptionally interesting series of Elizabethan or Jacobean wall paintings were rescued from the dormitories of the Deanery and transferred to the Cathedral for safe-keeping. By April the newspapers were reporting that passengers on the top decks of passing trams could view the progress on the building over the surrounding hoardings and by the middle of May 1904 the walls were built up to street level. Sixty-nine men were employed at the start, but this was to rise to ninety by the summer.

Charles Holden

ALTHOUGH THE COMPETITION FOR a new library had been nominally won by H. Percy Adams he was not the building's designer. This was the firm's chief draughtsman Charles H. Holden (1875-1960), a twenty-seven -year-old who had been with Adams since 1899. Holden was born in Lancashire and left school at the age of seventeen to work in his brother-in-law's architectural and surveying firm in Bolton. He then became apprenticed to E.W. Leeson in Manchester. During these three years he studied building construction at the Manchester Institute of Technology, especially concentrating on masonry and brickwork. Greatly talented, within a year of starting the course he was instructing students himself. Following a short stay in Bolton, Holden, then twenty-one, travelled to London to join Charles Ashbee, the noted Arts and Crafts designer and architect, who had founded the Guild and School of Handicraft in 1888. Ashbee was a passionate believer in craftsmanship in art and in bringing high quality back into everyday objects. The year spent with Ashbee opened Holden's eyes to the importance of good design and rounded his education. After a spell in Devon, where he pondered his future career, he joined the highly respected firm of H. Percy Adams, well known for designing hospital and office buildings.

Holden produced designs and collaborated on projects, providing new ideas to enhance Adams's staid elevations. He became indispensable and Adams made him a full partner in 1907. Apart from Bristol's Central Library, they designed the new buildings for the Bristol Royal Infirmary (1906-12), one of Holden's most innovative façades until it was masked by banal modern additions. Holden was a master at using and manipulating mass in architecture in order to create striking effects or to disguise height and size.

He was employed by the Imperial War Graves Commission intermittently from 1918 and then constantly between 1920 and 1926. It is, however, his designs for stations, street furniture and fittings for the London Underground that makes his work widely accessible to a great section of the public. His stations on the Northern and Piccadilly lines from the 1920s and 1930s show the influence of his visits to see the modern architecture of Scandinavia, Germany and Holland. Holden's most monumental building was the 1931-37 Senate House of the University of London.

This was a *tour de force* of his stripped classicism, with elements of American skyscraper style and rhythmic fenestration. Holden would continue to design buildings until the 1950s but his final years were given over to advising on town planning. When the Lending Library was revamped in 1956 he was invited to the opening celebrations on 20th June, exactly fifty years on from the initial ceremony. In a letter to the City Librarian W.S. Haugh, he declined the offer to make a speech saying he 'was more than pleased to take a silent part in the ceremony'. He further remarked that 'I am very retiring on such occasions and I prefer the building to speak for itself'. He did recall that his association with the planning and designing of the library had been one of the happiest memories of his life. After the ceremony Holden wrote again to Haugh, calling the replanning both impressive and charmingly carried out. He admitted that his Reference Library on the first floor probably now looked an antique by comparison and gave his blessing to any similar scheme to modernise that. A charming and self-effacing man, he twice declined a knighthood, saying that he wished to be excused because it would alienate him from ordinary people.

The Structure and Building Plan

HOLDEN'S LIBRARY WAS BUILT of brick faced in the best quality Hartham Park Bath stone. The chequer work was of green quarella stone, whilst the roof and other decorative tile features were of green Westmorland slate. The structure is supported by an internal framework of box-section girders, encased in mortar, and founded on individual massive blocks. The floors are constructed of iron and concrete, surfaced with either marble or pitch-pine blocks. This internal structure might almost be said to be separate from the external cladding, and much that appears to be structurally supportive is in fact merely decorative.

A competition requirement was that all parts of the building should be well lighted, so Holden employed skylights over much of the roofing area. The largest, over the Reference Library vault, is shielded from the street by the device of employing a shallow mansard roof so that only the outer slate-covered sections could be seen from the road below. This conceit also resulted in the building appearing to be much lower than it would have been with a conventionally pitched roof. The light well gave side light to stores and corridors around it but more importantly to the Lending Library which was directly below it. All over the library Holden employed glass partitions in order to capture every available piece of natural light in what was a very wide building. Panels of glass floor tiles known as Hayward's Lights were used in several areas of the building to spread natural illumination to the floor below. Unfortunately this system would function effectively only so long as nothing was done to interfere with it, but the changes in use of several sections of the building, and the covering of glass screens to effect privacy, soon made it ineffective. The Hayward tiles were unpopular with the female members of staff who imagined that male colleagues would be able to view them from below, and there was a fear of slipping on these 'non-slip' inventions. By June 1907 the architects were asked to come up with a solution. For a while, they were covered with rubber mats which proved a hazard in themselves, as did the wood-block floors that were so beautifully polished each morning. Holden employed electricity for the artificial lighting but gas was also laid on to some areas of the building and installed over the entrance doors in the event of an electrical failure.

The choice of Holden's plan for the new library was not welcomed by the City Librarian, Edward Robert Norris Mathews. Whilst not considering himself qualified to comment on the external attractions of the building he felt quite the reverse on the internal arrangements. He listed a catalogue of complaints and claimed that Holden had shown a 'vexatious disregard of the specified requirements', and stated that in his opinion the design was very far from being the best of the sixty one that were exhibited. Percy Adams therefore had to make some changes to the existing plans. Holden's fellow architects, however, seem to have been impressed by the building and remarked on his clever way of infusing the spirit of the old into the requirements of a modern library. Charles Marriott summed it up in *Modern English Architecture* of 1924, 'It emphasises the truth that the art of building is independent of period'.

Holden's first design for the north façade

Tudor rose decoration from the entrance door and,
far left, rainwater head

The Exterior

The Northern or Main Façade

HOLDEN SHOWED EXCEPTIONAL TASTE in designing his new building so as not to overshadow the Abbey Gatehouse. He drew upon the Gatehouse's general shape and elements of its decoration both outside and inside the new building. The library is actually a very large structure with six floors but the bulk of it is contained on the southern side where the land falls away. Setting the great vaults over the Reference Library back from the front parapet and breaking the angle of the gable, fools the eye into believing that in reality the building is the same height as the adjoining gatehouse. It is a tribute to Holden's skill that the building merges so well with its historic neighbours. His knack of drawing on historic references but creating something new from the past is shown to perfection in this assemblage of Cathedral, Gateway and Library. The façade is of Bath stone enlivened with quarella chequer work, reminiscent of that used by Holden in his design for the Midhurst Sanatorium.

Holden duplicated the mass and oriel of the gatehouse at either end of his main façade. The entrance door takes the place of the main Abbey arch at the eastern end whereas the western oriel is extended to street level by a rectangular bay and then is supported by a pilaster set between the arched tops of two of the basement windows. This bay differs from the published drawings of 1903 and 1905 where the western oriel sits rather clumsily on three six-light windows that are flush with the wall. The oriel parapets are lower than the rest of the front parapet, which allows the observer a good view of the circular windows and chequer work on the gables of the Reference Library vaults. A single arrow slit in these parapets alludes to the crenellations of the gatehouse. Almost hidden behind this central parapet are the windows of the upper Reference Library gallery. The façade with two projecting end 'towers' is suggestive of Charles Rennie Mackintosh's Scotland Road School in Glasgow of 1904, which it may have inspired, although the end oriels are there replaced by bow fronted towers. In Bristol the inspiration for the long oriels of the main façade must have been the neighbouring gateway, but they also remind one of C.R. Ashbee's 72-74 Cheyne Walk in London of 1897-8 during the time that Holden was employed by that architect.

Narrow six-light mullioned windows in arched recesses flank the oriels and portal at ground-floor level. Visually these take the place of the niched statue alcoves of the gateway portal and are repeated at either end of the central section of the façade. Six more windows of identical size but lacking the arched tops link these. Above them is the most innovative feature of the north front. Between and resting on shallow buttresses are suspended three high-waisted small oriels. Their fronts are ornamented with a lozenge of quarella whilst the flanking walls hold chequer work of the same stone. The published drawings show that below each of these oriels Holden had originally intended to hang some sort of cartouche or shield. Similarly Holden had not envisaged the shallow buttresses but had separated the windows by drainpipes, which were then moved to flank the large oriels and provided with spectacular corner lead rainwater-heads. These are castellated and decorated with pierced panels of ropework, heraldic flowers and inscribed A.D. 1905.

The Sculpture

What Holden had envisaged from the start was a series of relief sculptures in niches above the three oriels. The competition rules had specified that 'simplicity and breadth of effect are most desirable' and that 'the lavish use of ornament is to be avoided'. More lavish than his drawings at first specified, these niches were to be the focus of the main façade. The Bristol-born sculptor Charles Pibworth, 1878-1958, was also responsible for several statues on the Abbey Gateway. At Bristol School of Art, the Royal College of Art and the Royal Academy Schools he studied under such sculptors as Lanteri, Gilbert and Thorneycroft. By 1900 he was working in London. He collaborated with Holden on more than one project but this work is amongst his most impressive external displays. The twenty-one figures represent characters from early English literature. The eastern or first lunette on the left shows Chaucer and characters from *The Canterbury Tales*, ranging from the left: the Miller, the Merchant, the Wife of Bath, Chaucer, the Prioress, the Knight and the Man of Law. The model for the Prioress is said to have been Harriet Fricker, born in Frog Lane, Bristol in 1872 and reputed to have been related to Pibworth by marriage. Others on the façade may also have been family or friends. The central lunette shows the Venerable Bede and various literary saints. From the left these are St Aidan, St Chad, St Augustine, Bede, St Cuthbert, St Paulinus and Caedmon. To the right of the latter is an inscription 'C.Pibworth Sculptor. 1905'. The last lunette shows King Alfred and chroniclers. These figures are a minstrel, Cynewulf the wandering bard, St Gildas, King Alfred, William of Malmesbury, Florence of Worcester and Wace the Norman minstrel. Pibworth was to be paid £425 for the lunettes but he petitioned for, and was granted, an increase of £50.

Holden introduced more sculpture into his façade than is shown on the 1903 drawing. This was the work of William Aumonier after drawings by the architect. Aumonier (c.1839-1914) was the founder and head of Aumonier and Son of 84, Charlotte Street, London. He had worked with

Charles Pibworth's sculptures of Chaucer and the Canterbury pilgrims

The Venerable Bede and early literary saints

William Aumonier: emblems of the British Kingdoms and symbols of knowledge from the north-eastern gable

H. Percy Adams and Holden before on the Incorporated Law Society Building in Chancery Lane, and the Norwich Union Life Assurance Company's premises in High Holborn, London. The bottom of each of the large oriels is decorated with heavily carved panels of vines and grapes and branches loaded with figs, symbolic of the Tree of Knowledge, a more obscure artistic convention than the usual apple tree. Above the three small oriels is a charming decoration of rambling roses, an allusion to the Tudor roses of the Abbey Gateway. The building's gables are also ornamented although most are invisible from the ground. At their apexes shields hang from vegetal crests above scrolls. If originally destined to bear devices and inscriptions they were ultimately left blank. Down each side of the gables are three floral devices. Most common are the emblems of the United Kingdom, the Rose, the Shamrock and the Thistle, but others such as the pomegranate also occur at the rear of the building. Aumonier also carved the rebus shields on the outside of the staircase drum tower and the ropework on the rear oriels. Many years later, in 1939, Holden would commission Aumonier's grandson, Aubrey Eric Stacey Aumonier, to produce the great archer sculpture at East Finchley Station.

Throughout his career Holden engaged modern sculptors on his buildings, often in the face of furious criticism from his clients. As a member of the Art Workers' Guild he was friendly with other artists and knowledgeable about their work. He employed Jacob Epstein on several projects including the British Medical Association regardless of the hatred that that sculptor's work engendered in some quarters, and believed that sculpture should be integral to a façade and not an additional embellishment.

Southern, Eastern and Western Façades

Whereas the northern façade of the library is modern, yet low and picturesque, the other sides of the building show large modern vertical masses, which at first appear devoid of decoration. A study of the eastern and southern façades of the library shows that Holden based the major part of the structure on the tower keep of a Norman castle. The almost symmetrical right-hand section of the rear façade shows this most noticeably. Whether this Norman keep was an allusion to Bristol's lost Royal castle or just a suitable medieval cloak for a young architect to mask a large modern building juxtaposed to an ancient arch is impossible to say. Before the late addition of the oriels these façades would have appeared far more severe and the allusion more obvious. Two great 'corner towers', each with chimneys, poke above in the traditional place of stair turrets. The battlements of each tower are pierced by two blind crenellations and the uncrenellated parapet between them with its corbal table mimicking machicolations further refers to its original model. The three sets of clerestory lights of the top floor, behind the parapet, are interspersed with two three-sided projections. The pilaster buttresses are a common feature of Norman tower keeps such as Richmond, Castle Rising and The White Tower of London. The latter surely provided Holden with his inspiration for the row of decorative lunettes between the buttresses. High on the east façade may be seen a Norman arcade similar to those at Castle Rising and Corfe castle. Two of the four blind arches are pierced with the small rectangular windows that illuminate the top landing of the service stair. Behind this landing is the internal light well. The adjacent lift shaft protrudes from the façade and is pierced down its length by arrow slits, further enhancing the castle theme and making it resemble a tower keep's stair tower. The shaft now rises high above the parapet, but until the 1950s this was not such a noticeable feature of the roof line. To the north, a row of small windows follows the progress of the service stair up the building. A row of windows to the right of these was lost in the 1903 alterations to the plans. The pilaster buttresses are lower on this side of the building and have stepped tops. The two southern 'towers' of the east façade adjoining the lift shaft have a recess between them topped by a row of windows which light the top storey. Holden had proposed five narrower lights for here, but this was changed to four larger ones.

The bulk of the northern section of the building appears from the east as a plain, solid block of architecture. It rises behind the drum tower of the staircase in an almost windowless mass. The staircase drum sits between two great rectangular towers, again reminiscent of a castle keep but without the crenellations. The tops of these towers have parapets perhaps three metres deep and lined with lead. The drum tower's green slate roof rises between the blocks of the two rectangular towers in an exciting visual juxtaposition of geometric shapes. The great staircase's circular bulk ties together the rectangular masses of the front and rear of the building. Holden was obviously mindful of not detracting from the Abbey Gateway and it is a tribute to his skill and taste that the huge structure does not swamp the historic archway. He plays with structural features to create an interesting series of planes and relies on light and shadow to further enhance the effect. His seemingly bland wall at this northern section of the east façade is enlivened by wide stepped pilasters. The recesses caused by the latter are each topped by gently projecting parapets supported on short corbel tables, enlivened at a lower

Charles Rennie Mackintosh's Hill House with its stairtower and wings mirrors the mass arrangement of Holden's south-eastern corner of the Library. Photograph Robert Field

Mackintosh's revised 1907 western façade of Glasgow School of Art suggests a knowledge of Holden's work at Bristol. Photograph Robert Field

level with a decorative lozenge of green quarella. A chimney from the room above the western medieval arch was rebuilt and incorporated into Holden's façade here. The east façade is the one that differs most from Holden's published drawings following Norris Mathew's criticism and the expansion of the ground plan to the south, notably through the addition of oriel windows with bases ornamented with strapwork inspired by the decoration on the Abbey Gateway.

Three shields decorating the staircase tower are another detail borrowed by Holden from the neighbouring gateway. Again the work of Aumonier, they are all rebuses with designs based on bookbinding terms. Like all Aumonier's enrichments they were almost certainly Holden's idea. They show (from the right) a quart jug with an 'O' attached to the handle, which represents the term 'quarto'. Next is the front portion of a calf with a knife which represents 'half calf', and thirdly a sun with rays rising from a sea represented by a wavy band refers to the 'raised band' found on spines of some leather-bound books.

The profile of the Central Library as seen from the south-east next to the Cathedral School is so reminiscent of Charles Rennie Mackintosh's design for the south side of Hill House at Helensburgh of 1902-3 that one wonders if either architect was influenced by the other or if coincidence was at work. Certainly, Mackintosh's 1907 revised western façade for the Glasgow School of Art, with its high and sheer planes covered with oriels, suggests a knowledge of Holden's work.

The western end of the southern wing is treated quite differently from the eastern 'keep'. Here the allusion is domestic and the block resembles the end of a large Neo-Tudor mansion. The gable end of the Bristol Room with its great chimney is the most notable feature of the roofline. This chimney served the fireplaces of the caretaker's house and in theory that in the Bristol Room but the latter was never intended to be used. Its bold vertical mass increases the upward thrust of the building. A band of chequered work decorates the gable but otherwise the great mullioned windows and their surrounding shallow-stepped buttresses are the most striking decorative features of the upper part of the façade.

A delightful conceit that Holden added to the southern side of the building was the incorporation of a stylized house façade at this end to indicate the position of the maisonette where the resident caretaker lived. The little slate roofs and gable, with its quarella lozenge, cover the two bedrooms of the accommodation. The lower rooms consisted of a sitting room and a kitchen, with a scullery and lavatory to the side and rear. A deal staircase with ball-topped newel posts connected the floors. In 1908 it was decided to provide a 'front door' for the caretaker's apartments in the basement corridor separating them from the rest of the building. Holden annoyed the City Librarian by not using the whole of the available site and by providing a garden with lawns and flower beds. Mathews considered the plans for the library in consequence both curtailed and congested. Within a few months of opening it was found that part of the lawn was prone to flooding and the areas of concrete outside the south entrance were laid down. Holden's 1904 gabled and Romanesque-arched southern porch and bicycle shed were never built.

The western façade was composed of two distinct blocks. The southern section with serried ranks of great mullioned windows of different shapes and sizes, continued the domestic feeling of this part of the façade. The largest windows illuminated the basement stack whilst the

smallest lit the caretaker's staircase and his lavatory. The staircase had a four-light mullioned window and was where the 1967 glazed bridge now springs from Holden's building. The lavatory window below has lost its original leaded lights. Shallow buttresses were placed between the large windows on this side.

The northern section of the western façade mirrored that adjoining the Cathedral Arch at the eastern end with its corbel tables and wide shallow pilasters and quarella lozenges. It jutted out from the adjoining southern section but was partly masked by the Tyndale Mission. The chimney stack of the latter building was raised and the top built in Bath stone to merge into and rise above the library's parapet adjoining the most northern corbel table. In 1967 when the mission was replaced by the new extension, this chimney was lowered to the same height as the parapet and the lower brick courses were replaced in stone. The extension covered up far more of Holden's façade and the surrounding land than the mission previously had. This area had been occupied by a garage, workshop and an old coach house. A road dog–legged around the side of the mission and library. After 1967 two of these buildings in Lower Lamb Street that had formerly been the premises of Messrs Rowe Brothers became a furniture store for the library and a rented workshop. A railed staff garden by the side of the ramp to the underground car park survives slightly altered, although no longer in the library's ownership. The old coach house stood here. The southern wall of the garden incorporates remains of the abbey granary. The furniture stores and garden area were sold off by the County of Avon and converted into a theatre studio for the Cathedral School.

The Railings

The building was surrounded by railings in a restrained design of square 'nail-topped' bars. Whilst those at the rear and side of the building were simple stretches between Bath stone piers, those of the main façade abutted stanchions of wrought iron holding an elongated stylized device reminiscent of Holden's favourite circle within a circle. Here the design appears almost vegetal with its long attached 'stems'. The railings were painted blue-green to resemble bronze suffering from verdigris. When the 1967 extension was built a new stretch of railings to Holden's design was added to replace the old utilitarian ones of the Mission House. The stretches of railings on the south and east sides fell prey to the railing stripping mania of the 1939-45 war when the rear double

gates and eastern staff gate were also lost. Both gates seem to have been without ornament and designed to replicate the simple railings that flanked them. Considerable visual damage was done to the rear support wall in the post-war era when the central stretch had three of its piers removed and the wall was rebuilt in inferior style. It must be hoped that one day this wall and its gates will be restored to their original appearance. In front of the caretaker's house Holden replaced the railings with a stone screen wall to give privacy and its pilaster-like piers retain their original height. The screen wall also served to mask the difference in height between the ground level outside of the caretaker's house and the drop to the continuation of the railings and stone piers on the west side of the building. Here the railings remained in situ until the building of the extension in 1966-7.

The Entrance Stairs

The stairs that approach the main entrance form the roof of part of the bound-newspaper store below. These broad shallow flights are bounded by walls crowned with a simple wrought-iron railing and two iron lamp-standards designed by Holden. These elegant supports, made by Messrs Edbrooke after Holden's designs, are topped with balls and enlivened by restrained scrollwork. Originally Holden designed striking 2-foot (61cm)-high cylindrical iron, bronze and obscured opalescent glass lanterns to top them. These were made by the Thomas Street Brass and Copper Works in Bristol and fitted up for electricity by Buchanan and Curwen. The tops, which were dark bronze in colour, were pierced with the legend 'Central Reference Library' which would have been illuminated at night. These lanterns had been removed by the 1950s after which time they were replaced, first by contemporary street light shades and then (in the 1990s) by the anachronistic Georgian-style lanterns in imitation of those introduced to College Green at the same time. Holden was requested to design gates to match the railings within a few months of opening to protect the main doors after children had started climbing on them. The hand rails were added to the side walls after the 1970s.

The great escutcheon bearing the arms of the City of Bristol over the main doorway, was carved in situ by William Aumonier and links the bottom of the oriel to the entrance arch as does the less flamboyant example on the Abbey Gatehouse. The corners of the oriel are clasped by fruit-laden vines as an allusion to Dionysos, patron of Dramatic Art, and the fig-laden branches of the Tree of Knowledge. The door arch is decorated with a beribboned garland of bay laurel and berries, the sacred emblem of Apollo, god of the Arts, Eloquence and Useful Sciences. Below the missing fanlight the portal is framed by a modern design of stylized rose bushes and Tudor roses in an allusion to the Neo-Tudor of the library's architecture. The enlarged but still relatively small front door, whose size aroused criticism, may owe its proportions to the equally small portal found on Mackintosh's 1897 north façade of the Glasgow School of Art. Both the outer and the 1922 inner doors bear bands of hammered brass with repoussé inscriptions in an Arts and Crafts script 'The Municipal Central Library'. The original outer bands were possibly the work of Charles Ashbee's Cotswold Guild of Craftsmen who designed the silver ceremonial key for the building. In the 1980s these plates were replaced by facsimiles and the originals transferred to the store of the Bristol City Art Gallery.

The Interior

HOLDEN WAS OBVIOUSLY CONCERNED with spatial and lighting contrasts in his processional way from the front steps up to the Reference Library, which was the most important room in the building. The low and richly gloomy Entrance Hall opens on to the high and brilliantly lighted Grand Staircase, which itself leads to the low vaulted corridor approaching the high Reference Library reading room on the piano nobile. Apart from some of the fenestration the Medieval-Tudor inspiration of the exterior is largely abandoned inside in favour of the Classical.

The Entrance Hall

The Entrance Hall is almost Byzantine in appearance with its vaults, piers and lush use of marble and mosaic. It is approached from the street up a short staircase of white Sicilian marble from a vestibule floor of piastraccia and Irish green marble. The iron hand-rails are a post-1950s safety measure.

Originally the lunette above the entrance held a splendid stained-glass window. This, like the rest of the ornamental glass in the building, was by Benjamin Nelson. Unfortunately it was stripped out between 1956 and 1967 and replaced by a hardboard panel bearing plastic letters. From a surviving photograph taken from the exterior of the building it is possible to make out the main elements of the design and to suggest a colour scheme based on that of the room that it once illuminated and embellished. Like the building itself, the design was both modern and traditional, consisting of a central Art Nouveau panel of intersecting heart shapes formed by the stems of stylized rose trees. Tudor roses (found in the exterior and interior embellishments of the building) were prominently displayed in the pattern. The side segments flanking this were of styl-

ized trellis pattern around a lozenge shape. The fanlight echoes the shape of the mullioned thermal windows of the Reference Library corridor.

The Entrance Hall itself consists of a wide central walkway leading to the Grand Staircase that is flanked by narrower arcades. Those on the western side give access to the ground-floor departments. To the east, the arcades are extended with an additional row of piers and opened to the two oriel windows that were a late addition to the plan resulting from the expansion of the library floor plan to the south. They were presumably added not only to give more interest to the external façade but also to help illuminate what would have been a very dark room as Holden had originally envisaged only a simple six-light mullioned window here. The expansion also resulted in the rearrangement of the piers and pendentive vaults of the hall into the existing harmonious arrangement. The hall is clad in marble supplied by Walton, Goody and Cripps Ltd of nearby Canon's Marsh and fitted by the marble masons George Wood and Son of College Street. The floor is paved with piastraccia marble from Carrara, whilst the skirting or plinth is of Grand Antique.

The spectacular green wall and dado panels are of Greek cipollino marble and remind one forcefully of the painted imitations of this luxury stone that are so often found in ancient Roman wall painting. The capping rail is of Irish green marble from whence spring the vaults clad with mosaic work of turquoise vitreous glass.

An early photograph shows that originally the Porters' lodge to the left of the entrance approach occupied only the narrow space between the two eastern-most piers, where the ceiling is devoid of tessellation. The existing glazed door to this room shows just how cramped it would have been with barely space for the inmate to have sat down. A glazed

screen with four windows and a high marble-clad counter closed the room on the western side. Enquirers could speak to the porters through a casement window from a lobby area which matched that on the right-hand side of the entrance steps.

Today's brass chandeliers of the late 1980s replaced some of modern design installed in 1955. Originally the room was illuminated by three simple hanging shades in the form of brass-edged bowls of opalescent glass suspended from a brass ring attached to the ceiling. These, like the great electroliers of the Reference Library, were designed by Holden and conform to his favourite 'Saturn' design. Even when illuminated this room with its rich materials and low vaults would have seemed dark to the visitor and a surprising contrast to the staircase beyond.

The arches on the west side of the Entrance Hall were filled by glass screens resting on dado-high walls. The two doors in this screen nearest to the main entrance gave access to the News Room whilst the other opened into the Borrowers' Lobby for the Lending Library.

The Marble Staircase

The Sicilian marble stairs wind around the drum tower up to the first floor bounded by dado and walls of Bath stone. The height and brightness of the staircase is at first obscured by the wall facing the visitor which bears the coat of arms of Vincent Stuckey Lean, whose portrait may be seen on the landing above. It was his bequest of £50,000 that enabled the city to build this library. The family fortune was said to be founded upon banking, salt, trade and religion, and all these are reflected in the devices carved on the shield by Aumonier. The great south window bears stained glass by Benjamin Nelson showing the Arms of

Bristol flanked by the Common Seals. On the ceiling coving may be seen Tudor roses and the entwined monograms 'BCL' (Bristol Central Library) and the date 1906. Note that Holden has incorporated his ball-in-a-circle device into the 'o' of the date. The upper part of the wall above the plaster monograms is angled, producing an interesting geometrical vaulting for the ceiling. The arches of the landing overlooking the stairwell echo the windows of the corridor that the visitor approaches. The photographic portrait by H.A. Chapman of Stuckey Lean is a facsimile made from the original by Andrew Cotton of the City Museum. Chapman's photograph had used overpainting and the facsimile copies this technique exactly.

The impressive brass handrails are original to the building, and were probably extended as an added safety measure after 1955.

A separate flight of the Marble Staircase originally gave public access to the lower ground floor and the Specifications of Patents and Bound Newspapers Library. At night these stairs were illuminated between the window heads by half-cylindrical brass and glass wall lanterns vaguely reminiscent in design to the pair once on the entrance steps outside.

The Exhibition Corridor

At the top of the staircase doors give access to the marble-floored Exhibition Corridor. After the bright and spacious staircase the area of the corridor is by design, like the Entrance Hall, both lower and darker. The light comes via the building's internal light well. The style here is purely classical. The three thermal windows are copied from those used in the bath houses of ancient Rome, and indeed the architecture of this whole room refers to those establishments. Roman bath houses often included libraries for the benefit of their patrons. The low ceiling is heavily vaulted with three cross vaults between a pair of plain barrel vaults, allowing interesting play of light and shade. The cross vaults spring from eight staggered pilasters each bearing shallow aediculae or shrine-like niches on their façades. A heavy cornice runs below the vaulting and forms the arch of these niches. In 1906 the entrance to the Reference Library Reading Room was through the double doors half-way down the corridor. Holden had originally intended that the west wall of the corridor would be open to allow entry to the Bristol Room and Reading Room via doors on opposite sides of a narrow corridor on the site of the present Enquiry Desk. This idea flouted the Schedule of Conditions which stated that access to the Bristol Room was only to be through the main Reading Room and so he had to replace his western entrance with a blank wall. This became an exhibition space and in 1935 several Sheraton-style display cases were installed here and in the Entrance Hall. In 1967, when the new extension was added to the Holden building, the western end of the corridor was opened up to provide easy through-access and the old main side entrance became a fire door. Thus today the corridor is much as

23

Holden had intended it. To the right of the old entrance to the Reading Room is a bronze plaque of Holden by the portrait sculptor and medallist Paul Vincze (1907-1994).

The Reference Library

From the low corridor the visitor entered the high space of the Reference Library Reading Room. This is one of the grandest and most loved public rooms in the whole of the south and west. At first glance this most stately of rooms is also the most stolid and least adventurous of Holden's creations in the building. This however is misleading. With references to the thermal windows of the Exhibition Corridor, Holden obviously based this great room on the high chambers of the baths of Imperial Rome. The great tunnel vault of the ceiling is adapted into a skylight filled with square glass lights. They echo in shape the plaster panelling of the ceiling, whilst the lunette-shaped arches of the upper gallery that likewise echo the sculptural lunettes outside, take the place of the thermal windows one would expect to find in such a position on an ancient building. Circular windows composed of double thermal windows pierce the end and upper transept walls. Various academic libraries are said to have influenced Holden to design a classically inspired Reference Reading Room. However, the most likely inspiration may lie in the attached Holy of Holies: the Bristol Room, with its barrel-vaulted ceiling and Georgian details.

The Grand Opening of the new Central Library took place on 20th June 1906 and the official celebrations were held in this room. A dais was constructed at the western end for dignitaries and was backed by tall palm trees and fronted by a bank of foliage plants. Mr R.G. Chapman's Orchestral Band occupied the gallery above the dais and played a programme of operatic music before and after the municipal speeches. The local press were impressed by the building although the *Bristol Observer* criticised the lack of height of some of the rooms and coined a new word 'labyrinthian' to describe the effect of the corridors and passages on a stranger. The Library opened officially to the public on 25th June 1906.

The piers and columns visually supporting the ceiling and galleries in the Reference Library are actually of wood and plaster and are not load-bearing. Inside the piers and running up through the building is a framework of steel girders. Above the vaulted ceiling a network of steel and wooden girders bind the construction together and also support the vault. The apex of the roof above this framework is covered with glass to allow top-lighting. The piers supporting the vault are clad with pilasters topped by debased Ionic capitals of Holden's own design. The echinus (the moulding between the shaft and the top of the capital) of each pilaster is formed by a ribbon garland of Apollo's bay laurel, identical to that found on the entrance arch of the building. None of the capitals has any necking, the echinus taking a dual role. Between the volutes of the capital three wavy lines form another unique feature. Above the capitals Holden designed a bold entablature ornamented with dentils, but only the cornice continues all the way around the room. Flanking most of the Ionic pilasters at ground and first floor level are Tuscan columns which carry the gallery around the circuit of the room. Those on the first floor appear only between the four central piers and support the upper galleries and their lunettes. Holden provided each of the first-floor openings with a plaster frame that is joggled to catch the light on the architrave above each opening. The panelled parapet or balustrade that

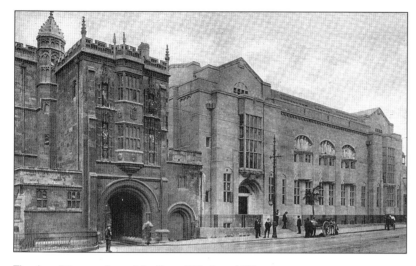

The day of the opening celebrations, 20th June 1906.
One of the palm trees for the dais is being delivered

runs around the gallery is actually a bookcase on its inner face and becomes a balustrade proper only in the area where the gallery walk leaps as a virtual bridge so as not to obscure the great oriels at either end of the room. Around the room at floor level the walls are lined with Tuscan pilasters, most noticeably at the east and west ends. The four pairs of double pilasters at either end of the room are each joined and turned into high triumphal arches by the insertion of a segmental arch into the entablature. Balusters continue the gallery parapet across the void and surmount a panel pierced by an oculus surrounded by short and heavy plaster swags. This arrangement not only serves to mask the iron spiral staircases but also forms an overdoor to one of the four staff entrances to the area once forbidden to the public. Originally no public library

Holden's variant of the Ionic capital

allowed open access to its books on the shelves. The public were expected to consult a catalogue or the staff and then wait for a particular book to be fetched for them. Until 1967, readers entering from what is now the fire door entered a small panelled lobby area created by the plain backs of extra large book presses. Thus funnelled into the room they would see a panelled enquiry desk directly opposite them between the columns. To judge by letters in the press the librarians on show to the public were all female. A letter in the *Bristol Observer* in November 1909 was typical in praising the qualities of the young ladies employed by the 'Stuckey Lean Reference Library'. They were 'simply perfect – no patronising, fawning, contempt, or weariness'. In the bays either side of the enquiry desk were large catalogue cabinets which effectively acted as a screen for the staff area behind. This section included the three small oriel windows. It had four large book presses spaced between the windows which made it seem less open than it appears today.

On the opposite side of the room the gaps between the columns were closed by two large radiators which survived until a renewal of the heating system in 2003. More book presses than exist today filled the area behind. Four cast-iron spiral staircases rose to the galleries above from the corners of the staff enclosures. Originally the pierced treads were open but the rubber was added as a safety measure in the 1980s. Holden designed four booklifts that worked on the counterpoise system to facilitate the retrieval of books from the book stacks on the upper floors. Only those at the west end of the room went up to the top gallery. They consist of two boxes, a pulley and a braking system. These still work but are no longer used as the area beneath is now public, and staff now have to carry books down the spiral stairs.

Large radiators also occupied the central gap between the columns at the east and west ends of the Reading Room and their removal in the 1960s was a great visual improvement. Both ends of the room beyond the columns were originally fenced off from the public by brass handrails supported on elegant Holden-designed Art Nouveau-style balusters. These were set between the columns and the fixing marks may still be traced on some and on the floor. Even the entrance-ways to the staff enclosure below the plaster swags were closed by a baluster and rail. These however were hinged at the side so that they could be raised for entry. The corral thus created at the western end became the lecture area for the library's successful series of monthly lectures that attracted many top authors and academics for almost fifty years. These started in January 1909 with a lecture by Professor Cowl on medieval poetry. One lecture on Lewis Carroll, in October 1936, attracted over 700 members of the public. After the First World War, weekly half-hour talks to children were also a successful feature of the winter months. This area was close to the Bristol Room, and the non-public lobby outside it, where the Enquiry Desk now stands, was provided with glass-topped display cases to show library treasures. Presumably both this area and the Bristol Room beyond were accessible upon application, and it appears that the central section of the brass rail here and probably elsewhere was hinged and could be lifted to permit access. That the brass railings did not deter the public from wandering into staff areas is illustrated by the fact that by September 1906 the City Librarian was grumbling that they were 'unsatisfactory'.

Originally Holden envisaged a more elaborate treatment for the upper part of the entablature of the Reading Room at the springing of the vaults. An early drawing shows seated statues or reliefs above each of the pilasters and flanking the railed lunettes of the upper galleries in the manner of Michelangelo's prophets and sibyls of the Sistine Chapel. Six were envisaged for each of the long sides of the room and six for each of the east and west walls.

Early in 1934 the Reading Room was opened out allowing readers access to the books on the shelves themselves. Early experiments with open access had started in the Reference Library in 1920 and Bristol was one of the first libraries in Britain to institute this novel idea. The work took three months to complete and involved the adding of new book presses and the reorganisation of others. The department was repainted at the same time and a photograph survives showing the room full of scaffolding below which life goes on with readers at the desks, and would be a modern Health and Safety nightmare. In 1931 the brass rails and balusters were removed from either end of the room and remodelled into guiding rails from the entrance up to an enlarged new island enquiry desk. The latter had been formed by joining the old enquiry desk with the matching catalogue plinths that had previously closed off the northern aisle. The new arrangement of guiding rails also served as a device for safeguarding the stock.

The Reference Library sustained some damage during the Second World War, but nothing as severe as the surrounding properties. In November 1940 an incendiary attack left windows and roof glass in the upper gallery broken. The adjoining Tyndale Mission, which had by that time become the Folk House, was almost destroyed by fire during a raid on 2nd December 1940, but the fire brigade managed to stop the flames from spreading to the library. In the same attack incendiary bombs penetrated the Reading Room and also the roof of what was the South Western Regional Library Bureau at the top of the south wing of the building. Damage was sustained by the skylights, roof, ceilings and floor blocks. The blast from a high-explosive bomb which fell near the main entrance to the library in the same raid increased the damage. On 3rd January 1941 another high-explosive bomb fell in Deanery Road close to the North Transept of the Cathedral and smashed some of the roof lights in the Reference Library, the Bureau and in the light well over the Lending Library. This also shattered windows in other parts of the building. The final raid that affected the library occurred on 11th April 1941, when a heavy high-explosive bomb at the rear of the building damaged windows, roof lights and tiles. Stone work on the south front was defaced in the blast and much debris was thrown on to the roof and over the top of the building into Deanery Road. First-aid repairs were made to the building and the library remained open. One item in a furniture inventory of the Reference Library made in 1941 is listed as 'a bomb snuffer'.

By the late 1950s the reader accommodation was proving embarrassingly inadequate with readers having to be turned away through lack of seating. In 1960-1961 the room was revamped in an effort to provide more space and light. The brass rails had already gone, but the enquiry desk was next removed, new lighting installed and redecoration undertaken. Tables were placed in the aisles where formerly, as now, there had been book presses and the radiators were removed or resited. The loss of the free-standing presses created problems for the accommodation of book stock in the room, although several new shelves were attached to the central oriels. The library catalogues were henceforth grouped together into the centre of the room. When the new extension was built in 1967 the area outside of the Bristol Room was glazed in on the north and east sides between the columns and it became a foyer to the new wing which was approached through openings pierced through the western bays. The eastern glass panel still survives. Photographic murals of the King Street Library and All Saints Church were attached to the walls as illustrations of the history of libraries in the city and three low circular tables and six chairs furnished it. In 2001 a new enquiry desk was constructed outside the Bristol Room.

The Electroliers

The greatest loss to this room was the removal and destruction of Holden's remarkable Saturn electroliers in the modernisation of 1961. There were originally six in the room, made of brass or brass-coated metal. Each electrolier consisted of two small 'planet' globes surrounded by rings which were interspersed with two elegant bobbin-like disks. Below these a huge spun-brass globe was suspended, boasting an encircling ring from which ten lights in opalescent shades hung. Similar shades still exist in parts of the Reference galleries. Below the largest 'planet' of each electrolier was a chain bearing another very small globe, a joined disk and planet and an end finial. Brass chains supported the whole construction. The original drawings for these lights have not been located, but from a quick sketch added to one of Holden's x-sections of the room it is obvious that it was his intention that the large circling brass ring of the biggest planet was to be level with the floor of the gallery. These electroliers again display the globe within a circle motif

Holden's ball-and-circle motif in the upper gallery ironwork

Holden's ultimate ball-and-circle design at Southgate Station. The roof standard is reminiscent of the library's electroliers

that obviously fascinated Holden and was to resurface later in his career. The design reminds one of the illuminated lantern on the roof of his remarkable Southgate underground station. There the actual building is a circle within a circle and the roof is topped by a lighting beacon of concrete rings, glass opalescent panels and a huge spun copper ball: basically the same idea one sees with these electroliers but turned upside down.

The Ironwork

Early drawings of the room show that Holden had not originally conceived anything modern or unusual in the way of ironwork to close the lunettes of his two upper-gallery book stacks. His final design, however, incorporated a central arched panel in a restrained Arts and Crafts style. This is flanked by simple bars relieved only where they meet the lunette walls by wrought-iron scroll filling. The whole arrangement is joined to an iron frame that encircles the lunette. What makes these railings of interest are the two standards that flank the centre. They are topped by a ring encircling a ball. Holden was to re-use this motif in 1931, but with the ball hanging rather than supported, in his design for lamp standards for Sudbury Town and other Underground stations. These rings on the railings are bolted to the encircling iron frames by a short length attached to their tops. Their origin may lie in a doodle Holden drew on a drawing for the entrance hall (RIBA Drawings Collection AHP (18) 63. 163), but he may also have found inspiration in the standards that Mackintosh added to the railings on his 1897-9 north façade of the Glasgow School of Art.

The Stained Glass

The great oriel windows at either end of the room hold many pieces of Benjamin Nelson's heraldic stained glass. At the west end (opposite the Enquiry Desk) the small coats of arms from left to right are those of Stuckey Lean, Edmund Burke, Sir Joseph Weston and William Wyrcestre. The larger ones below are, from the left, the Merchant Venturers and the Marquess of Bath. The window at the east end has the small coats of arms of Robert Southey, Robert Thorne, John Carr and The See of Bristol. The larger ones below are The Earl of Ducie and (to its right) the Duke of Beaufort. It had originally been intended to include the English scholar and humanist William Grocyn amongst the heraldry but it proved impossible to find his coat of arms. He was omitted in favour of Francis Fox whose shield may now be seen in the Bristol Room.

The Furniture

Holden was expected to design the furniture and fittings for the entire building, from conference tables to broom cupboards, and much of his work survives. In the Reading Room the ends of the book presses are copied in wainscot oak from those of the original King Street library. Possibly the fact that these were classical in design further prompted Holden to make the Reference Reading Room into a similar setting to the Bristol Room. Tops have been added over the years but his system of adjustable shelving still remains within them. In the galleries only the ends of the presses that were likely to be seen were given wooden ends, and these still retain their unroofed original appearance. The system of adjustable shelving, known as clutch stack, consisted of wooden shelves held up by rolled steel struts and brackets copper-electroplated to a rich bronze colour. Copper-plated pilasters for some of the end sections were provided and tubes ran above them linking the tops of individual presses together.

The two long reading tables for scientific periodicals and seven leather-topped study desks were of his design. The latter, which were known as 'special students tables' or 'cubicle tables', have been adapted for lighting which entailed removing their upper bookshelf, but are almost as he designed them. The leather writing surface of each was tooled with gold lines. When the desks were fitted with lights in 1961 an additional desk was added. It matched the older ones exactly and is only noticeable now because of the absence of any trace of the top bookshelf and the lighter colour of the teak. Holden's most interesting pieces in this room, however, are his two atlas tables in the bays of the great oriels. These have revolving tops and like most of the furniture designed by Holden in the building are of Moulmein Teak. The two revolving bookcases and the display cases have long gone. The former do not appear in any photographs of the Reading Room but may be seen in some early views of the Commercial Library on the mezzanine floor. The furniture was all made in Bristol by local craftsmen employed by the firm of Messrs Laverton, Webb and Co.

A large clock once stood on the architrave above the old entrance to the room and opposite the enquiry desk. It was a simple but elegantly designed piece with the face resting between two lyre supports and was in keeping with the room. The first clock supplied was criticised in July 1906 for being too small and was replaced by one with a 14-inch dial. It disappeared in the 1960s refurbishments.

The Bristol Room

This room was intended as a permanent memorial to the long history of public libraries in Bristol. It is a reasonably faithful recreation of the original first-floor reading room in the 1740 library in King Street using the oak book presses, panelling and fireplace from that building. The importance and classical feel of this facsimile room with its Georgian book presses and vaulted ceiling may well have determined the classicism of the main Reading Room itself where the presses were themselves copies of these. The original room had Georgian windows down each side and the fireplace was set between book presses rather than between windows. The cornice and barrel-vaulted ceiling, which echoes the shape of the great overmantel pediment, are in the spirit of the originals. At King Street, however, the ceiling was coved and was enlivened by a recessed rectangular central section from whence, by the end of the nineteenth century, two double gas lamps were suspended.

Henry Storer's engraving of the 1820s shows that at that date access to the King Street room was restricted by a latticed fence and probably gates between the third bookcases from the fireplace. Photographs taken in 1905, when the room was part of the Lending Library, show that by this time access to the presses was denied and the enquirer was channelled down the room by waist-high, heavy panelled screens. These were topped on either side by glazed library indicators which were attached to the presses by diagonal stays and raised the screen to almost six feet in height. It must have been exceedingly claustrophobic. The unfortunate borrower in search of a book was thus channelled down to a table behind which sat the librarian. Staff access to the presses could be gained only through two gates on either side of the main doors to the room where tall latticed examples appear in Storer's engraving.

Strangely enough from 1908 the Chief Librarian instructed that the doors of the replicated Bristol Room were always to be kept closed, which must have robbed the public of the view of the mantelpiece. In 1967 new glass doors were fitted in front of these so that the public could at last freely look into the room.

The Fireplace and Overmantle

The glory of the Bristol Room and one of the city's great treasures is the elaborate overmantel by the renowned English woodcarver Grinling Gibbons. On Gibbons's death in 1720 his studio collection was dispersed by auction the following year, and the overmantel bought by Alderman Michael Becher, at one time Sheriff of Bristol. Although no paperwork of this private transaction survives it is known that two chimney pieces by Gibbons sold at this sale for £100 and £120 respectively. Very little can be said with certainty concerning the acquisition. Mrs Becher told the Librarian, John Peace, in the 1830s that her relative had given it to the library after having purchased it at an auction. H. Avray Tipping in his 1914 book, *Grinling Gibbons and the Woodwork of his Age*, also suggested that it may well have come from the house built by Lord Berkeley of Stratton in 1665 which was burnt down in 1733. Tipping drew attention to the fact that this was only six years before Becher donated the overmantel to the King Street Library, which was then under construction. Against its being from Berkeley House is the coronet at the top and the monogram 'B. D.' In all probability this refers to the head of the family who was created Earl Berkeley and Viscount Dursley in 1679 and not Lord Berkeley of Stratton.

King Street Library in 1899. A watercolour by George Moore Henton

The main façade of Holden's library showing how the library harmonizes with its historic neighbour and inspiration, the Abbey gateway

The east façade. The library was first listed as a Grade I Listed Building in 1966

The southern façade in 1966 during the construction of the extension

The Pibworth lunettes

The eastern aisle of the entrance hall

The stair tower with its rebus shields in 1971

A reconstruction of one of the bronze lanterns from the entrance steps

A reconstruction of the lost Benjamin Nelson fanlight with Tudor rose motif over the entrance

The entrance hall

Benjamin Nelson's staircase window. The arms of Bristol flanked by the Common Seals

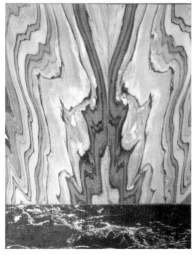

Cippolino marble from the entrance hall

Charles Holden.
The bronze plaque by Vincze, 1950

The west oriel with Nelson's glass

The Reference Library from the eastern bridge

Holden's ball-and-circle device in the ironwork of the upper galleries

Reference Library reading room

Clockwise from above

A spiral staircase and book lift on the gallery
of the reading room

The Bristol room in the late 1970s

Detail of the portrait presumed to be
of Michael Becher (photo: Stephen Morris)

View down the teak service stairwell from
the top floor

The arms of the Earl of Ducie in
the east oriel

Inside view of the galleon book den in the Children's Library

The 2004 revamping of the Lending Library saw the restoration of the 1906 mouldings and skylights

Since 2004 the Lending Library is again entered through doors in the former Newsroom's glass screens at its eastern end

In 2001 a café was created in the area of the 1967 extension previously occupied by the Library of Commerce

The Berkeley monogram
from the Grinling Gibbons
overmantel

The Annunciation from
a fourteenth-century
English book of hours

Treasures of The Central Library: the William Milton Collection

William Milton, 'A Book of Ornaments', designs for shop signs and trade cards c1710-1740:

Clockwise from above left

The Indian King

St George

Bristolia, goddess of Bristol

A leopard

The Indian Queen

Milton's work shows an astonishingly early and sophisticated use of the Rococo style in Bristol

The coroneted cipher in the pediment is surrounded by a vibrant display of wheatears and flower garlands: the latter form deeply projecting drops composed of flowers fruit and game, in the form of woodcocks ('real wood–cocks!', as the Librarian Rev Samuel Jackson was first to jokingly call them). Their presence suggests that the overmantel may have been designed for a dining room. Gibbons's speciality lay in carving groups and festoons of flowers, fruit, game and other ornaments as large as life and carefully copied from nature. He generally worked in softer lime wood so this creation in oak is particularly important. It is as fine as the similarly carved oak overmantels in the ground-floor suite at Hampton Court Palace. The projection of the carving of this overmantel exceeds those at Hampton Court and the groups are cut from single blocks here rather than built up in layers as at the Palace. The garland hangs either side of the central frame which holds a portrait on board of an unknown subject and by an unknown artist. It has almost certainly been with the overmantel since 1740. For many years it was believed to be by Jan Weenix (1640-1719), the Dutch game-piece painter, but the technique employed is quite unlike his and it could just as easily be the work of an English artist. The pilasters on which the curved pediment sits bear shallower drops of flowers and seed heads hanging from bows of ribbon, all most beautifully executed.

Photographs taken of the overmantel before its removal from King Street suggest that it was not varnished before 1906 and was presumably originally intended to resemble stone. In October 1905 the firm of Willcocks dismantled the mantelpiece and other fittings in King Street and repositioned them in this room at a cost of £2,000.

The fire surround itself is a marriage of odd pieces of carving that have nothing to do with Gibbons. The most interesting shows a section of what must have been a bipartite scene of the Judgement of Paris. The half that remains shows a reclining Venus accompanied by Cupid and Juno with her peacock. One male and two female putti play amongst them and hold a long beribboned Bacchic garland which issues from double cornucopias. Cupid points to the left and Juno turns her head in the same direction. They were once, no doubt, looking towards a disgruntled Minerva and Prince Paris of Troy, who would have been holding out the Golden Apple to Venus whom he had judged to be most beautiful of the three. As one of the oldest stories in the Western world the subject was a fitting choice for a library. This panel may have been reused from either another building or a ship, or salvaged from the earlier library building in King Street. It appears to date from around the 1690s. The two nicely carved amorino heads on either side of this panel are contemporary work and possibly by Paty or his sons. The hanging textile, although competent, is the weakest part of this ensemble. Originally the fireplace inside this wooden mantle was of simple but elegant moulded Bath stone which had been fitted with an iron grate. In 1906 this was not deemed exciting enough and a marble fireplace and turquoise glazed tiles replaced it. The present fireback shows Charity and is eighteenth-century. It may have come from King Street but is too big to have fitted into the fireplace as it was in 1900. The firedogs and basket are an Edwardian pastiche spuriously dated 1560 and display an odd collection of Biblical scenes from Samson with the lion and the gates of Gaza to David and his lyre and the Temptation. This room and the area immediately outside it, where the Enquiry Desk is now situated, were for many years used as the museum of the library and manuscripts and incunabula were displayed in cases

down the centre. The collection of local history books and maps is now housed here. This followed the donation of the Braikenridge collection of historic Bristol prints and ephemera in 1908. In the time of the City Librarian George Pryce (1858–1868), Bristol was the first city library in the country to establish and maintain a special collection of literature relating to its history. In 1906 the room housed the literary collection of the building's founder Vincent Stuckey Lean. Also included were the collections of Archbishop Tobias Mathew from 1613, the John Heylin Collection (donated in 1766) and that of the Rev. Alexander Catcott of 1799. Apart from these, the important collection of Hebrew and German literature presented in 1904 by the widow of the Rev. Naham Nürnberg of Bath was also included.

At the outbreak of war in 1939 many of the Library's treasures, manuscripts, early printed books and the Emanuel Green Somerset Collection, had been taken to a bomb-proof location away from the building. On 24th November 1940 an incendiary bomb damaged the roof and ceiling of this room. The only damage was the loss of a pair of blackout curtains and a withdrawn copy of an English dictionary that had been left on a desk.

The Furniture

The 1740 book presses in the Bristol Room are likely to be designed by James Paty I. They were originally fitted with unglazed cupboards at the top. These were still in place in the 1820s when Henry Storer published an engraving of the room but had been removed by 1900. The infills where the hinges once were may still be seen. Books were originally shelved in them by size, with the smallest volumes at the top. They were

King Street library. Grinling Gibbons's fireplace before the move to the new building

then arranged alphabetically by author. When the presses were moved, Holden was asked to fit a modern system of adjustable shelves within their carcases. The cases were also rather strangely given the names of those connected with the past history of the service, for example Robert Redwood and George Pryce. These were painted on the stretchers between the top two panels of each of the presses's ends. Originally the room was supplied with central electroliers, presumably in the same position that the gas lamps had been at King Street, but by the summer of 1906 these were deemed unnecessary and the Librarian complained that they obstructed the view of the overmantel. Each press was afterwards fitted with individual lights that hung down from curved metal brackets placed in the centre of each side, but these were removed by the 1950s. The glass doors were fitted to the presses ten years later.

The seventeenth-century upholstered chair by the side of the fireplace is traditionally said to have been that in which Judge Jeffreys sat during the Bristol 'Bloody Assize' of 1685. Jeffreys lodged in King Street during this period and was thus a neighbour of the library, so there may well be fact in the legend.

The eighteenth-century fan-back Windsor chairs are to be seen in Storer's 1820s engraving and are believed to have been in the room since the previous century. Following the introduction of Windsor chairs to the Bodleian Library in 1766, such seating was deemed suitable for 'ornament and repose' in other libraries.

The Neo-Classical sideboard table is said to have been thrown from the windows of the Mansion House in Queen Square during its destruction in the Bristol riots of 1831. It was acquired by the library shortly afterwards, most probably at the salvage sale. Considering the age and respectability of the Librarian at that period, the story that he had 'liberated' it from Queen Square after the riots is probably fanciful. The damaged top was restored with a veneer in 1906 that has not faded like the original. The folding library steps are believed to date from the Edwardian period and may have been the work of the Cotswold School. Mathews requested several small ladders or steps for this room in May 1906, so they may indeed date from this period.

The Stained Glass
The heraldic glass in the Bristol Room by Benjamin Nelson commemorates on the left-hand side of the mantelpiece (from the left) the local historian and book collector Alderman Francis Fox, J.P. and Archbishop Tobias Mathew, and on the right of the mantelpiece (also from the left), Bishop Butler and Edward Colston.

The City Librarian's Office
An inner and outer door give entry and privacy to this room through the east wall of the Bristol Room. The outer one bears a very fine ram's head coat hook which was presumably part of the King Street fittings. This office is a double-aspect room, looking over Canon's Marsh to the south and the central light well to the north. Holden designed virtually everything from the conference table, with its Tudor rose drop handles, to the matching side table, chairs and the glazed bookcase. The City Librarian's desk was originally a fine roll-top model and traditionally stood in the corner of the room next to the built-in pigeon-holes. It was unfortunately sold to a private buyer in the 1980s. Originally the room also accommodated a chesterfield and two men's easy chairs, all covered in red

morocco. One of the latter survives in the padded swivel chair. A 19-foot square 'Turkey carpet' was supplied to lie in front of the desk and also a rug for the fireplace. Both appear in the foreground of the 1906 staff photograph. Drawings in the R.I.B.A. collection show that the fireplace and overmantel underwent changes before the present design was decided upon. The elegant striking clock was bought for the room for £4 10sd from the Bristol Goldsmiths' Alliance at the same time as the other clocks in the public departments. Two lesser offices completed the southern wing beyond this room.

The Second Floor

The southern gallery of the Reading Room is wider than that on the northern side as it extends over the Exhibition Corridor. It is illuminated by windows overlooking the light well and also by skylights, and forms part of the second floor of the building. The roof forms a sun terrace on the outside of the building at third-floor level. A fact that has irritated several generations of sun-worshipping librarians is that Holden never thought to include doors to this terrace which is practically inaccessible. The southern gallery is said to be haunted. The apparition is a monk, presumably still searching for the lost dormitories of the Deanery. Other librarians with neat classifying minds have placed this apparition in the gallery above, where many books on theology are stored. He has not been seen for many years.

Originally the whole of the second floor surrounding the light well was open-plan and devoted to shelving for the Reference Library books.

The Third Floor

This was originally an open-plan book stack on four sides of the light well. The southern range was brilliantly supplied with natural light from windows on all sides and from skylights above. The floor had large panels of Hayward's glass prismatic pavement tiles so that light would be reflected down to the book stack below. On the outside the row of small windows on either side of the south wing are topped by a cavetto moulding and appear almost ancient Egyptian in style.

This room became the Patents' Store in 1920 and, between 1937 and 2005, the headquarters of the South Western Regional Library Bureau for inter-library borrowing.

The Ground Floor: The Lending Library

Originally the Newsroom, the Magazine Room and the Lending Library occupied the ground floor. These departments had little architectural ornament beyond a blind arcade at the western end of the Newsroom and a moulding that ran around the walls and piers at the level of the first horizontal window mullion. The arcade was pierced in 1967 to reach the new extension. The moulding was removed in 1956 but replaced by a lighter one in 2004 which now continues into areas that were once unornamented. The original moulding's profile survives on plans drawn up in 1923 for a screen across the Magazine Room. At the southern end of the latter a blind arch added some interest to the wall. The handsome oriels, were, in 1906, not visible to the public and within the book store of the Lending Library because of their late inclusion into the plans. The eastern one was flanked by a pair of narrow arches and these, together with the oriel in the south wall, form one of the building's most charming architectural corners.

Holden's vision for this floor aroused great opposition from the City Librarian who complained to his Committee that the provision on the ground floor was out of all proportion to that actually needed. He accused the architect of giving first consideration to this floor rather than to the Reference Library which was the *raison d'être* for the building. He criticized the amount of space awarded to the Lending Library at the expense of the then important Newsroom, which he termed 'cramped'. Norris Mathews further objected to the Newsroom being on the northern side whereas the Lending Library bookstore occupied the sunny southern portion. He prophesized that the sound of the trams in Deanery Road would be distracting as would the passage of borrowers through the central door in the south screen. More serious was his criticism of the lack of staff work areas provided. He suggested that the Lending Library be raised several feet to allow staff a good supervisory view of the public and Holden acted on this. The *Bristol Observer* on viewing the new library on 24th February, 1906 criticised the low ceiling on this floor, doubting if enough light would reach the centre of the building on dull days.

The Lending Library of 1906 was not an open-access collection where the public could browse the books. From the Entrance Hall the borrower entered the Borrowers' Lobby through the southernmost set of doors in the glazed screen. Before Norris Mathew's criticisms a wider lobby was planned and a narrower Newsroom. When Holden enlarged the ground plan, he was able to realign the north wall of the Borrowers' Lobby further south, thus increasing the size of the Newsroom. Elements of this original Borrowers' Lobby survived until the 2003-4 refurbishment by H.B.S. Architecture but are now masked by this replanning. For illumination this lobby was fully glazed between the piers on the northern side to match the Entrance Hall screens. The Lending Library counter ran along between the piers on the southern side of the lobby. Following Mathew's proposals this department was raised 15 inches above the rest of the ground floor to enable staff supervision and a step was provided to enable smaller readers to reach the panelled teak counters. One counter was labelled 'Issues' and another 'Returns' in gold letters.

Twenty-five thousand lending volumes were housed on this plateau in 24 book presses arranged in serried ranks north to south. These would have been identical in appearance to those remaining in the Reference Library Gallery. The eight presses in public view were provided with 8-feet high ornamental oak ends, based on those in the Bristol Room. Apart from having windows on all sides, the book store was brilliantly lit from above by three large skylights in the bottom of the central light well. Their walls were panelled to match the counters. Below, and in between the book presses, the floor was pierced with nine long strips of Hayward's Lights to illuminate the basement. The counters housed six Bristol Library Indicators, manufactured in Bristol by A.S. Scull of Redcliffe Street. Listing accession numbers of books in the catalogues, they indicated to the public whether or not that title was on loan. The borrower first located the title in the catalogue and then wrote out a request slip on the writing slope attached to the glass screen opposite the central counter. This was provided with five chained pencils. Having checked the indicator to see if the book was available they would enquire at the counter and, on the production of a brass library tablet, would be allowed to borrow the book. The librarian would then amend the indicator. Five of the indicators for books held 5,000 numbers each and a smaller one for magazines and reviews, 3,000. Standing on the counters and flanking the piers that rose up through them, they allowed contact with the staff through the intervening gaps. Three glass-fronted catalogue frames stood on the western counter. The public were each allowed one tablet which enabled them to borrow a single book. For the payment of a penny they were allowed a second tablet with which they could borrow one non-fiction item. The Annual Report of 1908-9 classified the occupations of borrowers to the numbers of books borrowed in ten categories. The greatest number were borrowed by students, juvenile readers, warehousemen and assistants, followed closely by working females.

The new ceilings both here and in the Reference Library, caused considerable trouble in 1906. Continual fractures resulted in the return of workmen and so much dust that £25 had to be spent on cleaning the books and shelves before the library could open. The City Librarian also requested that female staff be compensated for injury to their clothing.

Women and the library service

Limited employment opportunities for young women in the early twentieth century led to severe competition for posts. Applicants had to be between the ages of 15 and 18 and were expected to take part in periodic elementary examinations set by the City Librarian. They needed ability in handwriting, dictation, arithmetic, geography, English history and literature. The successful applicants were chosen as positions became available according to the number of marks they had achieved. It was not uncommon to have a four-year waiting list for a vacancy.

Wages ranged from 8/- weekly up to 21/- according to merit and length of service. Norris Mathews in a speech recorded in the *Western Daily Press* of 14th July 1897, stated the accepted view that women, for all their excellence, having less in the way of 'personal expenses or worldly responsibilities', required less in the manner of wages than men and were thus cheaper to employ. Unlike many authorities, Bristol was a pioneer in allowing female librarians and had permitted young women of education and respectable parentage to be employed in the city since the Public Library Act of 1876. It was, however, considered necessary that they give up any thoughts of matrimony and devote themselves instead to their profession. No married woman was permitted to work in the library. Bristol was also a pioneer in bringing a hierarchical approach to the profession of Library Assistant with the staff graded by title. With such a high proportion of female staff, it was inevitable that there should be trouble during the vibrant days of the Suffragettes. In June 1913 Launcelot Acland Taylor, the Deputy City Librarian, wrote in a letter about a recent incident concerning 'traitorous and underhand action' by a female member of staff, and lamented the fact that several women, egged on by 'the dominating personality of one of their members' and imbued with 'advanced suffragistic ideals', had recently joined the National Union of Clerks and were demanding increased wages. He claimed that the 'insidious forces' at work demanded drastic treatment. That resentment did not cease, however, is evident in a round-robin petition sent in May 1915 to the Libraries Committee by most of the female staff requesting 2/- per week extra during the war because of the rise in everyday living. They reminded the Committee that the male employees had already been awarded a sum. The devoted servants who signed this

The entire library staff in 1906. Norris Mathews and his deputy, Launcelot Acland Taylor, may be seen in the centre

petition were awarded their two shillings with the addition of a shilling war bonus.

In 1917 the ground floor of the Library was handed over to the National Recruiting Committee; offices were inserted in front of the oriel windows and a reduced lending service continued in the Entrance Hall and the Reference Library.

1920s Changes

In 1923 the Lending Library was converted to an open-access system. The first stage of this innovative scheme involved the transfer of the juvenile literature into a new Children's Library in the room on the mezzanine once used as the Patents Library and later as the Library of Commerce. The Bristol interior-fitting firm of George Parnall & Co. were called in to change the layout of the Lending Library plateau. The counters were removed and joined together to form a pentagonal issue counter. Their original places were filled by an elegant teak classical trellis that for the most part survived until the refurbishment of 2004. From the centre of the Borrowers' Lobby steps led up to the new counter through a wide balustraded approach. Gates attached to the counter signalled the places of entrance and exit. Parnalls left the original panelling at the bottom of the old counter's piers but continued it around to all four sides. The original metal book presses had been 8-feet high but these were clearly too tall for public use. Parnalls were asked to make new book cases using, and no doubt adding to, the original Holden ornamental oak ends but shortening them by a foot in height. Thus the presses that we see today in the library have elements of 1906, 1923 and 2004 in their design.

Recent Changes

By 1950 the Lending Library was looking antiquated and could no longer provide sufficient space for readers. The decision was taken to move it into the larger space occupied by the Newsroom and the Magazine Rooms. In 1955 the City Estates Surveyor drew up a plan for the reorganisation of the ground floor. The area on the higher level previously occupied by the Lending Library was provided with new shelving that split it into two distinct sections. The eastern one now housed the Library of Commerce, whilst the western became a department called Special Collections, which encompassed Music, Drama, Local History, books in

A typical evening in the new Children's Library in the mezzanine room in 1924. Vases of flowers on the tables were provided by the children

foreign languages and Braille. The redevelopment altered the central section of the west side of the plateau where there had once been the enquiry desk for the Magazine Room and built it up to the same level as the rest of the Special Collections area. In the north-west corner a new stair replaced the balustrade whilst the old central entrance-way of the 1920s was blocked by reused balustrading; a new stair inserted between the first and second piers gave access to the Library of Commerce.

In 1967 the Library of Commerce moved to the west end of the extension now occupied by the Children's Library and Café and became known as the Library of Commerce, Technology and Science. The Special Collections moved east and became the Music Library. The skylights were obscured by sheets of pierced white plastic at ceiling level. Their removal in 2004 marked a great aesthetic improvement. The Music Library flourished and was staffed by a team of specialist librarians offering expertise on all matters pertaining to the musical arts. A collection of gramophone records for home loan became the forerunner of today's audio-visual collections.

Considerable interest among all levels of society in the city led to the establishment of a specialist arts department in the site vacated by the Special Collections. The Fine Art Library was founded in 1967. The 1950s shelving layout was slightly modified and a through-way established between the Art and Music libraries by the removal of the most northerly bay of the dividing shelving wall. The shelving itself had to be altered to accommodate the large size of art books. Both specialist libraries were for reference and borrowing. The Fine Art Library, virtually unique in the south of the country, spawned several imitators. It was to amass one of the finest lending and reference book stocks outside London, encompassing all aspects of the non-performing arts and, amongst many related subjects, covered handicrafts, antiques and collectables. It had three specialist staff and in its thirty years became one of the best loved and highly regarded of the public departments. It closed as a separate department, amidst public protest, in 1997 during a series of economic cuts. Although many lending volumes were lost from the department then, the incomparable collection of art reference volumes, together with the former Art Librarian, now flourish on the first floor.

A new entrance ramp to the Art and Music Libraries at the front of the Parnall balustrade in the 1980s entered the Art Library by the middle pier of the old Borrowers' Lobby. With the revamping of the ground floor in 2003-4 the ramp for disabled access was inserted in the area that

The Fine Art Library in 1979 showing the floor with three panels of Hayward's Lights

had once held the Library of Commerce enquiry desk and the Holden book presses were remodelled, to be placed more or less in their original positions on the plateau.

Magazine Library

Originally known as the Reading and Magazine Room or the General Reading Room, this department occupied the south-west section of the ground floor below the plateau of the Lending Library. It was provided with four 14-feet long tables for adult readers and three slightly smaller ones for juvenile readers, who had to be ten years old before they could use the Magazine Room and Lending Library and fifteen for the Reference Library, unless granted special permission. They formed the third largest group of library users in the Edwardian city.

The department had several novel features when first opened. A recessed section on the east side where the access ramp now is, was set aside for a quick reference, open-access collection of books. This open-access collection was a daring experiment in its day and was generally not abused by the public. Thefts occurred, however. The first from the collection occurred in December 1907 and in the following Christmas books were stolen and newspapers cut and damaged. Things seemed to be getting worse by February 1909 when Mathews reported that 'vicious and degenerate persons' had been writing obscene remarks in publications. On 18th February 1910 during an electric light failure both the *Electrical Times* and the *Electrical Review* were stolen in the resulting gloom. In fact thefts of library books were surprisingly rare in Edwardian times but one detected incident in 1904 had seen the thief sent to prison for six months. Apart from periodicals displayed on tables and in racks,

readers could request books from the Lending Library to read here.

With the end of hostilities in 1919, the room entered a new era. Norris Mathews died on 4 January 1919, having been City Librarian since 1893. His place was taken by Launcelot Acland Taylor, who had been Deputy City Librarian since 1905 and was a strong advocate of open-access libraries and business information. Through his efforts, a Library of Commerce was founded in 1920 in the old Patents Library on the mezzanine which transferred in 1923 into the Magazine Room. This involved building a glazed screen across the room from the pier adjoining the open-access recess (which became an enquiry desk), and installing new shelving. This space was soon found to be totally inadequate and in 1932-3 the floor space was almost doubled by moving the glazed screen to run level with the north wall of the Borrowers' Lobby.

In 1955 the department moved to a new site on the plateau whilst this area became part of the Lending Library. The enquiry desk recess disappeared, being raised to match the rest of the plateau, whilst the screen, moulding and electroliers were also removed.

The Newsroom

Before the age of radio and television the newsroom was a most important department in any library. Opening hours exceeded all others in the library; thus here, it opened at 9 am and closed at 10 pm. Unlike the Lending Library, which was closed at 2 pm on Wednesdays, and the Reference Library which closed at the same time on Fridays, the Newsroom, Magazine Room, and the two rooms on the mezzanine were open daily. The range of publications taken by the department was huge by today's standards with over sixty newspapers as well as magazines and journals. Bristol Library was surprisingly modern and liberal, rejecting the witch-hunt against betting that had seen some libraries blacking out the horse racing results in a moral crusade against gambling.

It was entered by the two sets of doors to the right of the main entrance. The spaces between the piers on its southern side were closed by a screen of glazed panels above a plain dado, doors here allowing access to the Lending Library. Lighting was supplied by spindle-shaped brass electroliers with elements of design similar to those on the first floor.

Holden designed some old fashioned-looking newspaper reading stands as he was required to match those already in use at Bristol branch libraries. Fifteen were supplied and took two newspapers each side. The slopes were fitted with brass newspaper restrainers supplied by the Library Ads Company.

Shortly after January 1907, each stand seems to have been fitted with two pairs of brass reading lamps. Four reading tables, similar to those in the other newsrooms, and a directory stand were designed. Two magazine racks stood in the arcade at the west end. Mathews advised his committee in December 1905 that although the specifications had invited the architect to design the furniture, better examples were to be found in some of Bristol's newer branch libraries. Drawings and photographs of these lost pieces by Holden remain. On the west wall a large clock kept time above the blind arcade.

On 1st February 1918, the Newsroom opened to the public as the recruits' reception room for the Ministry of National Service. In the following year, the newspaper stands returned from their temporary home in the Entrance Hall and for a while the room continued unchanged. However, the transfer of the Commercial Library to the Magazine Room engendered the first of many alterations. In 1926 the whole building was closed from May 3th to 17th during the General Strike and was used as the recruiting headquarters. In 1932 the Commercial Library screen was moved northward to the place where the temporary Headquarters Office wall had been in 1918. Soon afterwards the newspaper stands were dismantled and their tops transferred to reading slopes to clad the north and south walls. Brass reading lamps were placed at about every ten feet

The Newsroom in 1932, prior to alteration

above the slopes and six long tables occupied the floor. The effect was to make the room seem far more spacious and light, although the slopes below the windows obscured the lower panes of glass and slightly spoiled the effect.

During the Depression the use of the Newsroom was phenomenal with 9,500 visitors to the City's newsrooms in just one day. Use of all of the Library's facilities rocketed and the staff realised the importance of their service to the unemployed.

In 1940 an air raid badly damaged the old Council House and the Exchange in Corn Street, and the Town Clerk's and Rates Department of the City were transferred to the Central Library. A small office was built into the north-west corner of the newsroom whilst a north-south counter was placed across the room from the fourth pier from the entrance. The Newsroom accommodation was thus halved. The Rates Department finally left the building in 1955 allowing a complete revamping of the ground floor.

The services given by the Newsroom, the Newspaper and Patent Library and the periodicals in the Reference Library were combined into the Newspaper, Periodical and Patent library. This opened on the lower ground floor where the 1906 Patent Library had been and consisted of the two rooms linked by a service counter where an arch had been cut through the east wall. The layout and counter, decorated with wooden stripes, were designed by Peter Heaton. This design-conscious librarian was responsible for the purchase of several pieces of high quality furniture through the progressive firm of Ganes of College Green. At one time laminated tables by Alvar Aalto were commonplace in the building. Unfortunately all but one of these have been sold off in recent years. The reading slopes from the Newsroom were redeployed to provide space for sixteen newspapers and teak benches cannibalised to form individual stools. Two of the original Newsroom's long teak tables, and a couple of the circular ones from the 1930s were also re-used and survived until 2001. The glazed screens of the Borrowers' Lobby were dismantled, opening up the whole floor as one space. The Children's Library now moved up from the lower ground to the space just inside the original entrances to the Newsroom. This department was provided with its own enquiry desk and a bank of north-south shelving delineating a rectangular space. It was to stay here until the access work of 1999-2001 ousted the Library of Commerce from its 1967 location. Then the department moved to its present location at the west end of the building.

A new issue counter was constructed for the Lending Library from the old one which had previously been part of the 1906 furnishing. Until recently, libraries threw very little away that could be remodelled by the City's carpenters. This new island counter flanked the north side of the old Borrowers' Lobby, which now became the only entrance to the floor. The most striking feature of the remodelled counter was a huge kidney-shaped canopy suspended above it and containing lights. It was a dark raspberry colour and was both oppressive and hot to work beneath.

The original hall doors to the Newsroom were removed and delightful glass screens inserted. Sandblasted and coloured, these showed a map of branches in the City and a directional guide to departments in the building. Above them were the coloured heraldic arms of Bristol. A very pretty glass screen with sand blasted stripes surrounding a white beribboned panel holding the City arms and the legend 'Central Lending Library' in red lettering was attached to the east side of the main counter. All these panels were taken down and stored in the 1970s during the Avon County Council period but have recently been destroyed.

The Holden shelving was removed from its original location and placed in the Newsroom and Magazine room areas. New shelving below the windows was too high and again masked their proportions. More seriously, the 1955 reorganisation destroyed the heavy moulding rail that had ornamented the walls and piers since 1906. Most of the piers now had display shelving clad about them at dado level and this was further

enlivened below by a 'V'-shaped decoration of white rope bought from a ship's chandler in Park Row. The rope was threaded between the skirting board and the shelves and was a playful and novel allusion to Bristol's maritime heritage. It had only a brief life. Well designed modern furniture, contemporary lighting and a slightly alarming, but mostly light, colour scheme all added to the modernity of the new Lending Library.

The extension of 1967 was joined to the old building through the previously blind arcade in the west wall. At the same time a strangely old-fashioned glazed librarian's office made of reused material was inserted into the north-west corner of the room, remaining there until 2003 when disability-access work completely changed the layout of the Lending Library once again.

The Lower Ground Floor

The eastern staff entrance gives access to this floor which in 1906 consisted of a kind of a glazed gallery around the basement void. From the start, the narrowness of this entrance led to delivery problems with furniture. On entering the building one passes on the left the women's lavatory and the office that was once the female staff room when the sexes were segregated. Beyond this the long administrative office was originally the Distribution or Unpacking Room where new books would be catalogued and distributed to the city's libraries. Next were the bedrooms of the caretaker's house and its staircase to the basement. The row of glazed offices on the west date to 1956 and predate the inserting of the mezzanine floor of 1957-9 above the basement.

Basement

In 1906 the basement was a vast open bookstore for 10,000 volumes reaching up to the Lending Library. It was illuminated by long windows and from the glass screens of the mezzanine. Hayward's tiles in the ceiling below the light wells gave further light. On the southern side a glazed corridor gave access to the male lavatory, mess room and boiler room. Beyond these, to the south west, were the downstairs rooms of the caretaker's house with a scullery, kitchen and living room.

The Patent Library

This room and the adjoining Bound Newspaper Library occupy a rather strange plateau within the building, being neither in the basement nor on the lower-ground floor. It has a northern and rather dreary aspect across the area facing the wall that supports the viaduct bearing Deanery Road. The City Librarian criticised Holden for putting this and the first-floor public departments on the northern side of the building rather than on the sunny southern side. It is not known why Holden chose to place these rooms at this level, although a true basement position would really have been untenable both for lighting and aspect. The cross sections of the building show that the piles for girders here are at a higher level than the rest of the building which suggests that the shelf of underlying rock was not excavated. Possibly this was through fear of undermining the adjoining Abbey Gate or in order that the curve of the lower flight of the Marble Staircase could reach it without another spiral.

From the staircase one entered a glazed lobby. To the right were the double doors to the Bound Newspaper Library whilst straight ahead were the doors to the Patents Library. Apart from the mullioned windows this room had no decorative ornamentation. Glass screens around the top of the south and west walls allowed light to percolate into the basement. A somewhat parsimonious attitude towards lighting in these lower rooms was displayed by a regulation issued on 16th August 1906 that only one light might be lit in the Patent and Bound Newspaper libraries, unless members of the public were present. All the new shelving in this room suddenly collapsed in September 1907, fortunately without casualties. In 1917 the room was appropriated as a war-time mess and the patents moved to the top of the building. The room became the

Library of Commerce in 1920 with its stock displayed for public perusal. Its analytical catalogue of articles in the 130 periodicals taken by the department was one of the finest in Britain.

In 1923 the Commercial Library moved to the ground floor and the following year the Children's Library was established here. Less furniture and formality, frilled glass-lampshades and a few framed children's pictures gave the room a slightly friendlier feel. During the war the room was occupied by the Town Clerk's staff, reopening in 1946, redecorated and with easy chairs and small tables. The book stock was returned from the Central Lending Library. The room remained the Children's Library until 1956 when it became the Newspaper Library and was joined to the Bound Newspaper Library by an arch. The Newspaper Library was installed with a reading slope for journals, which still remains, and two 1906 long teak tables which were unfortunately sold in 2001. The reading slope is adapted from those that once ran around the original newsroom, and which was itself built from Holden's original news stands. Thus another element of Holden's designs survives, at least in part. The Newspaper Library closed through staff shortages in 1997 and has not reopened, because of lack of disabled access. Many periodicals were also cancelled at this sad time which also saw the dismantling of the subject departments and the evening closure of the building on two nights a week. In 2001 it was converted into a general office for senior librarians.

The Bound Newspaper Library

This room was approached through the doors to the right of the marble staircase. The whole of the southern side of the room is a fully glazed work room, at the rear of which a strange raised stage-like semicircular structure is part of the support for the marble staircase above. The main features of the Bound Newspaper Room, however, are the huge fireproof 'bins' housing the collection of bound newspapers. It was envisaged that 2,000 such volumes would be kept here and the cases were made in sections to be assembled in the building. They are made of cold rolled, pickled and annealed steel, strengthened by rods hidden within the interior construction. The steel was finished with four coats of green enamel, each baked to a hard finish and then rubbed down with pumice stone and oil between coats. The shelves beneath the window housed the Patent Abridgement volumes from 1917 until the 1950s. Somewhat confusingly the name of the Department was then changed to the Patent Library.

The Service Stairs and Lift

The floors of the Holden building are connected by the teak service staircase that runs up through the six floors of the building. Originally there was merely a book lift to take volumes to each floor. The Committee decided that an electric lift was an extravagance and so plumped for a manual one. This was prone to break down and one of the pre-opening problems faced by the staff in 1906 was that none of the booklifts in the building was working properly. In 1959, the lift was replaced with a small passenger car which would enable both books and staff to be carried between floors.

The 1967 Extension

Clarke's design for the north front of the 1967 extension. The top floor was never built

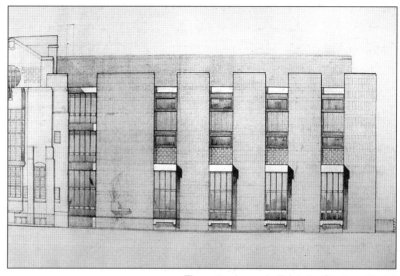

BY THE LATE 1950S it was obvious that the Holden building could no longer cope with the demands of an increasingly popular library service and the growing number of specialist demands that it was now expected to meet. In 1959 the chance to acquire the old Tyndale Mission site arose and the Council purchased it. The City Architect, Albert H. Clarke, was instructed to draw up plans for the extension. Planning approval was granted in April 1964 and the detailed scheme given Council approval in June. The building was estimated to cost £224,500. Even in the architecturally bleak 1960s it was realised that the Holden building was one of great charm and distinction and that any extension must be designed with great sensitivity. The Fine Arts Commission was consulted and construction started in 1965.

Apart from relieving the problem of inadequate seating in the Reference Library the new development was primarily aimed at the creation of new subject libraries in Art and Science and Technology and the expansion of the existing subject libraries in Local History, Commerce and Music. The new building would also provide a study hall and research rooms for the Reference Library and a considerable amount of new book storage in the basement. Clarke and the associated architect Francis Hannam of the firm Burrough and Hannam managed to produce a modern design that drew on elements of Holden's building just as the latter had drawn on the Abbey Gatehouse for his.

The new extension as built was phase one of what was to be an ambitious project. In judging its architectural merit one must realise that only part of the planned structure was actually built. From the start it had been thought highly desirable that the new building should on the top floor include an auditorium for lectures, musical and theatrical performances

The extension as built (photo: Stephen Morris)

51

and conferences. The 1957 report visualised the theatre seating 300 and having a gallery. This would have enabled the Reference Library to continue its long standing series of lectures, which had been discontinued through lack of space, but it was also to provide a suitable venue for dramatic performances allied to the library's drama collection. The auditorium gallery and School Library Centre would occupy a floor above the Reference Library extension. Clarke's façade with its chequer work and hanging oriels was intended to be equal in height to the existing building. His drawing of the projected façade shows a second row of rectangular windows above those now existing. These would have finished at exactly the same height as the top of the parapet of the great western oriel so that the eye would have been led effortlessly from old to new. The wall was to be finished as now with the large toothed crenellations but originally these were to finish level with the top of the parapet wall supported by the corbel table. Finally the bulk of the building was, like Holden's, set back from the façade and would have been level with the top of the supporting wall of the north-western gable of the Reference Library.

By 1964 the theatre had been reduced to a single floor and had been designed so that it could be added later if funds were available.

The final part of the scheme envisaged building a new wing behind the library on the west side of College Square down to Anchor Road. Unfortunately this area was sold off by Avon County Council in 1996 in the last days of its existence.

The new extension was opened to the public on 10th July 1967. Apart from boasting a small but useful sub-basement car park it was four instead of the original projected five floors high. The basement housed book stacks, a photographic room, stores and a headquarters for the Schools Library Service. The latter was later moved to Bedminster and the room became the Cataloguing and Acquisitions Department. The lower-ground floor was provided with an administration office, a new laminating room for book processing, a private office, book store and staff lavatories.

The ground floor of the extension held the impressive new Commercial Library at its west end. The rest was devoted to an expansion of the Lending Library. Both this and the floor above were provided with high ceilings and were spacious modern rooms. The furniture was again designed especially for the building as had been the case with the Holden building. On the first floor the Reference Library was almost doubled in size with a large south reading room, housing the collection of books on ancient, foreign and English literature. This room also functioned as an events room and an exhibition display area. It had great reading tables specially made for it. There was also a collection of study carrels and a workroom. In the main this arrangement stayed until 1997 when the Reference Art Collection and enquiry desk were moved into the north-west corner of the South Reading Room.

Recent Improvements

WITH THE DISCOVERY OF ASBESTOS in 1999 the 1967 building was closed to the public. The Bristol firm of Architecton, fronted by Colin Harvey, were brought in to transform the ground and first floors after the asbestos had been removed and the first phase of what was to be a £1.6 million project was begun. When the extension was reopened, the Children's Library had moved into the space historically used by the Commercial or Business Library and the north-western part of the area was now a café. The Children's Library was provided with a large book den in the form of a galleon designed by Mark Amis in honour of Bristol's maritime heritage. A new suspended ramped entrance was now abutted to the western side of the extension, allowing easy access to the building from Deanery Road and a new passenger lift with attractive glazed vestibules, replaced the 1967 one. Ceilings were drastically lowered on the first floor and bright colour schemes introduced. The South Reading Room, its furniture, study carrels and workroom were all swept away and became the Learning Centre and Disability Centre. The former is the latest transformation of the Library of Commerce but with less emphasis on books and more on IT. Two new windows were introduced at this time into the western façade of the building which had previously had none.

The redecorated and reorganized extension re-opened to the public in two stages in 2001. The first floor opened on 18th May, following the installation of forty computers funded by the People's Network. The Government's New Opportunity Fund provided the city with £600,000 allowing Bristol to be the first library service in the south-west to offer this facility. The ground floor was reopened on 25th October and on 23rd November received an official visit from the Princess Royal.

This revamping left the Holden section of the ground floor both shabby and less accessible to the disabled by comparison. In 2002 £320,000 was granted to the Library Service by the City Council's Sustainable Development & Social Justice Committee to improve disabled access to this section of the building. HBS Architecture were appointed to re-plan and execute the improvements. Urgent structural repairs were first carried out to the oriel windows and ceiling of this floor. Apart from the redecoration, refurnishing and installation of accessible counters and a wider wheelchair ramp to the raised area, the new scheme included the enhancing and replacing of several original features of the building such as the skylights and the moulded dado rail in the Lending Library. Both the new lighting and the new low-level shelving, along with a number of restored original 1906 shelving units were arranged in a grid that carefully reflected the gridlines of the Holden architecture. All these improvements together with the increased lighting and a sensitive colour scheme opened up the body of the room and prepared the building to face a new century as a modern library. The Lending Library fully reopened to the public on 5th April 2004.

Praised and admired by the architectural world since its opening in 1906, Charles Holden's Bristol Central Library has also become very dear to the public at large. A 2002 survey to mark British Architecture Week conducted by the Bristol Architecture Centre and supported by the *Evening Post*, saw it voted Bristol's most popular twentieth-century building. After a century this fine example of the Edwardian Free Style continues to function and to draw new admirers.

Further Reading

Early history to 1906

ARROWSMITH

Dictionary of Bristol. Bristol, 1906.

WILLIAM BARRETT

The History and Antiquities of the City of Bristol. Bristol. pp.507-8.

BRISTOL PUBLIC LIBRARIES

Annual Reports. Bristol.

BRISTOL PUBLIC LIBRARIES

Bristol Libraries Cuttings. 1876-1899, 1899-1904, 1905-1906, 1907-1912.

BRISTOL CITY LIBRARIES

Bristol Free Libraries Librarian's Reports, 1893-1906. Manuscript.

DENING, C.F.W.

The Eighteenth Century Architecture of Bristol. Bristol. 1923.

EVANS, Rev. John

The History of Bristol. Bristol. 1816 pp.270-273.

HUGHES, W. W.

'Mural Decorations in a Dormitory of the Old Deanery, College Green, Bristol'. Proceedings of the Clifton Antiquarian Society for 1900-1903. Vol. V, 1904, 147-153.

Full-size facsimile copies of the murals survive in the Reference Library Collection. (B2915-2920 location M14)

MATHEWS, E.R. Norris

History of the Bristol Library. Bristol. 1906.

ORME, Nicholas

'The Guild of Kalendars, Bristol'. Transactions of the Bristol and Gloucestershire Archaeological Society. Vol. XCVI, 1978, 32-52.

Bacchic putto from the fire suround below the Grinling Gibbons overmantel

PRIEST, Gordon

The Paty Family: Makers of Eighteenth-Century Bristol. Bristol. 2003.

TAYLOR, John

The Earliest Free Libraries of England. St Helens, 1886.

TIPPING, H. Avray

Grinling Gibbons and the Wood-Work of his Age. London. 1914.

TOVEY, Charles

A Free Library for Bristol. London. 1855.

The Holden Building and beyond

AN AGREEMENT made between Laverton Webb and Company Ltd and The Lord Mayor, Aldermen and Burgesses of the City of Bristol for...fittings and furniture. Bristol. 1905. (Reference Library acc. no. B21713)

BARNES, H. Jefferson

Charles Rennie Mackintosh. Ironwork and Metalwork. Glasgow. c1969.

BEESON, Anthony

Bristol Central Library, College Green. A Miscellany of Articles. 1997. Manuscript.

BEESON, Anthony (compiler)
Bristol Central Library. Historic Building Files. Loose-leaf files of articles and photographs. Manuscript.

BLISS, Douglas Percy
Charles Rennie Mackintosh and the Glasgow School of Art. Glasgow. 1979.

BRISTOL PUBLIC LIBRARIES
Annual Reports. Bristol. (after 1931 known as Reading in Bristol).

BRISTOL PUBLIC LIBRARIES
Bristol Libraries Cuttings, 1907-1912.

BRISTOL PUBLIC LIBRARIES
Bristol Free Libraries Librarian's Reports. Manuscript.

BRITISH ARCHITECT
'The Bristol Library Competition'. British Architect. 3.4.1903. illus.

BUILDER
Bristol Central Reference Library. The Builder. 2.9.1905, p255, illus.

BUILDING NEWS
The Bristol Central Library. The Building News. 17. 4.1903. p545. illus.

CITY AND COUNTY OF BRISTOL
Proposed New Central Library. Schedule of Accommodation and Requirements.
Bristol. 1902. (Reference Library Acc. No. B28499).

CITY AND COUNTY OF BRISTOL. PUBLIC LIBRARIES.
The Bristol Library. Bristol. 1956.

CITY AND COUNTY OF BRISTOL. PUBLIC LIBRARIES.
Chief Librarian's Instructions to Staff. Bristol. 1906 Mss.
(Bookstack F).

CITY AND COUNTY OF BRISTOL. PUBLIC LIBRARIES.
Proposed Extension to the Central Library. Bristol. 1957. Mss.

FOYLE, Andrew
Bristol. Pevsner. Architectural Guide. New Haven and London. 2004.

HAUGH, W. S. (editor)
A Brief History of the Bristol Public Libraries. Bristol. 1953.

HOWARTH, Thomas
Charles Rennie Mackintosh and the Modern Movement. London. 1977.

KAROL, Eitan and ALLIBONE, Finch
Charles Holden. Architect 1875-1960. London. 1988.

LAWRENCE, David
Underground Architecture. Harrow, 1994.

LEBOFF, David
London Underground Stations. Shepperton. 1994.

LIBRARY BUREAU LTD.
Tenders for furniture. To the Libraries Committee, City and County of Bristol. London 1905. Mss (Reference Library Accession No B28499)

MARRIOTT, Charles
Modern English Architecture. London. 1924.

MENEAR, Laurence
London's Underground Stations. Speldhurst. 1983.

REILLY, C. M.
'Charles Holden'. Building. September. 1931. 396-401.

SUTTON, A. R.
Bristol Central Library. 1983. Mss (Reference Library Accession Nos. SR37 & 727.8 ARR).

THOMSON, George
Central Library, 1934-1974. Reminiscences. Manuscript. 1980.

ARCHITECTURAL PLANS AND DRAWINGS

The most comprehensive assemblage of plans, drawings and furniture designs referring to the Central Library is now kept in the Royal Institute of British Architects Drawings and Archives Collection, Henry Cole Wing, Victoria and Albert Museum, London. They possess the large office archive of Adams, Holden and Pearson together with personal Holden memorabilia presented to the RIBA in 1999 by Holden's great niece.

In Bristol itself the majority of plans and drawings relating to the building are to be found at the Reference Library, College Green, Bristol. This collection includes photographs and drawings of the building from all periods.

The Bristol Record Office at B Bond Warehouse, Smeaton Road, Bristol has a number of plans of the building and some furniture designs at ref. 103. 07785(70) A-G and another set in BUILDING Vol. 46. Minute books of the various Council committees are also a great source of information and may be found here. Prior warning should be given as the retrieval of some material may require several days' notice.

Superior schoolboy poseurs seem to have been a feature of the post-war Children's Library